# I'VE PUBLISHED MY BOOK, NOW WHAT?

**STEPHANIE A. WYNN**

**Copyright © 2022 I've Published My Book Now, What™**

All rights reserved. No part of this publication may be reproduced, distributed, or transmitted in any form by any means, including photocopying, recording, or other electronic or mechanical methods, without prior written permission of the publisher, in writing from the publisher, except in brief quotations embodied in critical reviews and certain other noncommercial uses permitted by copyright law. For permission requests, write to the copyright holder addressed "Attention: Permission To Reproduce I've Published My Book, Now What™ Book at **stephanieawynn.com**

ISBN: 979-8-218-02309-6

ISBN: 978-1-0880-4217-5 (E-Book)

Library of Congress Control Number: 2022917286

First Printing Edition 2022
I've Published My Book, Now What
A Simple Guide To Establishing A Successful Author Brand

PO BOX 1344
St. Petersburg, FL 33731

# Disclaimer

This book provides information on entrepreneurship only. This information is provided and sold with the knowledge that the publisher and author offer no legal or medical advice. In the case of a need for any such expertise, consult with the appropriate professional. This book does not contain all information available on the subject. This book has not been specific to any individual people or organizations' situations or needs. Reasonable efforts have been made to make this book accurate. However, there may be typographical and or content errors. Therefore, this book should serve only as a general guide and not as the ultimate source of subject information. This book contains information that might be dated or erroneous and is intended only to educate and entertain. The author and publisher shall have no liability or responsibility to any person or entity regarding any loss or damage incurred, or alleged to have incurred, directly or indirectly, by the information in this book or because of anyone acting or failing to act upon the information in this book. You agree never to sue and to hold the author and publisher harmless from any claims arising out of the information in this book. You agree to be bound by this disclaimer, covenant not to sue and release. You may return this book within the guaranteed period for a full refund. In the interest of full disclosure, this book contains affiliate links that might pay the author or publisher a commission upon any purchase from the company. While the author and publisher take no responsibility for any virus or technical issues that could be caused by such links, the business practices of these companies and or the performance of any product or service, the author or publisher has used the product or service and makes a recommendation in good faith based on that experience.

All characters appearing in this work are fictitious. Any resemblance to real persons, living or dead, is purely coincidental.

This book is dedicated to my parents, Diane and Sam, and my sons, Brian and Jamie. Thank you for always being there for me. Stay Gold!

# Contents

Foreword ............................................................. ix
Introduction ....................................................... xi

Chapter 1: The Need For A Growth Mindset ... 1
Chapter 2: The Importance Of An
 Author Brand ................................. 7
Chapter 3: Book Marketing 101 ..................... 15
Chapter 4: How To Set Your Book Apart ........ 21
Chapter 5: 5 Reasons Authors Give
 Up On Their Book ....................... 28
Chapter 6: How To Position Yourself
 For Publishing .............................. 34
Chapter 7: Believe In Yourself ........................ 38

Author Terms ...................................................... 43
Author Resources ................................................ 49
Author Brand Checklist Template ..................... 55
Author Book Signing Pitch Template ................ 57
About the Author ............................................... 59
Index ................................................................... 61

# Foreword

It has been my pleasure to know Stephanie Wynn in a friendship that has gone from a mere acquaintance and professional colleague to a partnership in writing. I have watched Stephanie unveil her passion for pushing the underrepresented forward and sharing her gifts and talents in a way that is imminent and validated in the pages of this book. After battling with her own setbacks and misfortunes, she remains faithful and obedient to Christ. She uses her ***own*** journey to formulate an easy-to-read and step-by-step guide as she willingly divulges demonstrated tips and unhidden truths about building a brand to be successful.

This book's premise reminds me (*and probably many first-time completers of things*) of when I graduated with my first degree and thought, "Here I am, world, I am prepared to do it all." But when the job offers didn't pour in, and the rejection letters piled up – I could relate to the title of this book.

In *I've Published My Book, Now What?* Stephanie has crafted a simple, straightforward guide for aspiring authors and emerging authors who need to execute their dreams and examine their full potential. She takes the reader through a series of questions that home in on the specifics of each person's journey accompanied with *to-do's, how-tos,* and accountability checkpoints. She does so with openness, honesty, and matter of fact. After reading this book, the only thing stopping you will be you.

—D. MICHELLE KINDRED, Professor of Education, substantive editing and consulting, author, and philanthropist

# Introduction

Congratulations! If you're reading this, it means you're either interested in publishing a book or have gone through the publishing process.

My name is Stephanie A. Wynn. I will provide you with some great tips and resources to create a successful author brand. Writing a book can be exciting, overwhelming, and a little discouraging at times, but with careful planning, effort, and time, your book, your brand, and your business can be successful.

I've had several successful business ventures: an ice cream shop, a cleaning business, and a coaching business. Even though these are different endeavors, I discovered they all needed a marketing plan and strategy. Instead of reinventing the wheel and doing things I wasn't sure would work, I applied simplistic branding, marketing, and business development concepts that worked.

Before embarking on your *authorpreneurship* journey, it's important to get laser-focused and mentally prepared to put forth effort and time. You must go in with the clear understanding that writing a book is more than just book sales. Remember, if nobody knows you exist as an author, nobody will be interested in buying what you are selling.

# Chapter One

# The Need For A Growth Mindset

*"And be not conformed to this world: but be ye transformed by the renewing of your mind, that ye may prove what is that good, and acceptable, and perfect, will of God."*
—Romans 12:2 KJV

There are two types of mindsets I will cover in this chapter, Fixed Mindset vs. Growth Mindset.

One of the biggest roadblocks to writing a book, succeeding as an author, or achieving goals is having a FIXED mindset.

Individuals with a Fixed mindset are often described as set in their ways and resistant to change.

People who think this way often place limitations on themselves and believe their lack of success is primarily due to various external circumstances.

This mindset causes your talents to be "fixed," meaning you can't be improved or enhanced.

A fixed mindset is a form of self-sabotage that increases your probability of failure.

Individuals with a growth mindset can be described as believing their talents and abilities can be further developed through hard work, dedication, and a positive outlook. Thinking this way allows room for self-improvement, increasing their probability of success.

Having a Growth Mindset is the key to success. Those with a fixed mindset may feel they can't change, but that's not true. Thankfully, individuals with a fixed mindset can shift to a growth mindset with these tips:

1. **Discover a sense of purpose.** Individuals with a growth mindset look at the big picture and have something to strive for.

2. **Stop using the word "fail."** Few children learn how to ride a bike without falling. Babies fall constantly until they can walk. Both Amazon and FedEx took years to become profitable companies. The same logic applies to trying something new. Keep trying until you succeed.

3. **Stop looking for approval from others.** Some "friends" will frown upon your ideas out of spite or because they have a closed mindset and don't understand what you're trying to accomplish.

4. **Use others for inspiration.** Juxtapose of #3, learn from those who have succeeded at what you're trying to accomplish. Discover what they did and emulate them.

Remember: if they can, you can too.

5. **Find a mentor.** Befriend someone who has achieved success and ask them for advice. Unlike #3, a good mentor will help you achieve your goals, not deter you or tell you it's impossible. Before looking for a mentor, truly understand your intentions before asking someone to mentor you.

6. **Focus on the journey, not the destination.** Many of life's greatest lessons (and memories) come from the journey, not the *final* destination.

7. **Silence the inner voice.** As fixed-mindset thoughts enter the mind, they must be immediately silenced with positive thoughts: "I can do this." "It may be difficult, but it's not impossible." "I will accomplish my goals!"

8. **Learn everything you can about building your author brand**. Continuously learning new ideas and strategies is essential to growth, which is crucial to having a growth mindset. No one knows everything.

9. **Discover your talents.** Everyone has their own set of unique talents and gifts. Unearth yours and focus on improving them.

10. **Learn from your mistakes**. Use your missteps as learning tools. Instead of letting them defeat you, make adjustments until you reach your goal.

If a person has a growth mindset, anything is possible, as success starts from within. If your goal is to sell 1 million copies of your book, it begins with a thought in your mind, and second, you <u>must</u> write it down. Changing your mindset will bring you one step closer to achieving your goals. To grow within any industry starts with the renewing of your mind.

**Chapter Takeaway:** Moving forward or becoming a millionaire will require changing your mindset from being fixed to a growth business mindset.

**Chapter Affirmation: I WILL CHANGE THE WAY I THINK!**

# Chapter Two

# The Importance Of An Author Brand

*"Your brand is what other people say about you when you are not in the room."*
—*Jeff Bezos*

To succeed as an author, you must be unique and stand out from your competition. The goal is to create a distinctive style that will define you as an author. One way to do this is by establishing your brand.

Having a brand is as essential as an author because it allows you to connect with your reader audience personally. Your brand will be the foundation of your *author* business and your success. Why? Because this is how you will inform your *reader audience* of who you are, it will make it easy for them to bond with you.

Before building your author brand, you need to understand the difference between a brand and branding.

**A Brand** is the physical aspect of your platform, which includes the website, logo, and marketing tools such as flyers, business cards, etc. Your brand will be how your ideal reader audience identifies and differentiate you and your book from your competition.

**Branding** is putting your platform in front of your ideal audience. It's your product and or service, the method of communication you'll use to connect with your readers. It's implementing strategies that will draw in your readers. It's an organic ongoing conversation you will have with your potential and existing ideal reader audience.

I have found that most authors think they need to promote their books to increase sales. This is slightly true; before promoting the book, you need to build an author brand. So rather than promote your book, you'll promote your author brand. And when your ideal reader audience is connected to your author platform, they'll buy whatever you sell them. Know this; your brand is the vehicle that drives business sales. So that means no brand equals no sales.

At 23, I started my first Ice Cream Shop. I had no point of reference, nor did I have a brand. Social media didn't exist. You had to market your business manually. I enrolled in the Entrepreneurship Academy offered here at the local city Chamber of Commerce, and there I learned the importance of building a solid platform for your business, creating a business plan, and creating a solid brand.

Remember, your brand is how your audience identifies you, and it's your message to express who you are and what you represent. Let's look at how to build an author brand.

# How To Build An Author Brand?

*"Branding is the process of connecting
good strategy with good creativity."*
—Marty Neumeier

Brand and Branding are important terms to understand when you're building your author brand. To create a solid author brand, here are things you will need to start the process.

**Effort & Time:** Building your author brand requires two essential items needed to succeed, Effort and Time. Do not invest your money if you cannot put forth effort and time.

**Financial Investment:** At some point, you must invest in your brand. I would recommend getting three quotes from three vendors who work with integrity, someone who you can trust and deliver on what they say.

**Create a Marketing Strategy or Marketing Plan:** You will need to plan when, where, and how you will market your brand. This plan also includes financial investment. Before receiving the physical copy of your book, create a plan of action for your book, your brand, and where your business is going?

**Build Your Email List:** You will need to build an email list to keep your audience updated on what is going on with your book, your brand, and your business's branding, publishing, and marketing process.

To create an email list, you can choose from the following email marketing software:

- Mailchimp
- Convert Kit
- Constant Contact
- Mailer Lite

**Create A Signature Logo:** An author signature logo is a must-have. Here are a few tips to consider when creating your author signature logo:

- **Make it difficult to forget:** Your logo is the first thing your ideal reader sees with your business. Your logo is what makes you memorable. For example, when you see Starbucks or Chick-Fil-A, you immediately understand who and what you will get from these organizations. The goal is to create a logo that people will not forget.
- **Keep the colors modest:** Keeping the colors simple and the detail not too intricate

will help your logo appear the same everywhere it is used. Your logo may appear on various platforms (television, billboards, print media, clothing, pens, etc.). Too much color or too many features may appear distorted or look differently from one media type to the next. Keeping it simple is key.

- **Use it everywhere:** Put your logo on everything related to your business. It will take time for people to remember you or take notice, and brand recognition is key.
- **Author Business cards:** These could be digital or paper cards. There are many templates out there. (Resource: Hackstack App) You can download the app Hackstack in your app stores. Once you have a logo, it's time to create a business card. Keep it super simple. The front of your card should have basic information in a quick, easy-to-read format:
  o  Logo
  o  Your name
  o  Title
  o  Contact info (address, phone number, email address)
  o  Website
  o  QR code (optional)

Before promoting your book to your ideal reader audience, create a marketing plan and strategy first.

**Chapter Takeaways: Implement the following right away.**

1. Create a brand message that is clear, concise and stands out.

2. Develop social media templates that support your author brand message.

3. Consistently market your author content to your reader audience on your platforms.

**Chapter Affirmation: I WILL NOT FAIL**

## Chapter Three

# Book Marketing 101

*"Everyone is not your customer."*
—Seth Godin

Marketing can be a bit intimidating if you are unsure what you are doing. No worries, during this chapter, I will break down how marketing works simplistically. Let's jump right in.

**What is Marketing?** According to Webster Mariam dictionary, Marketing is the process or technique of promoting, selling, and distributing a product or service. Marketing constitutes the big picture of how a company plans to raise awareness of its brand and convince customers to make a purchase.

When you hear the word Marketing, what comes to your mind?

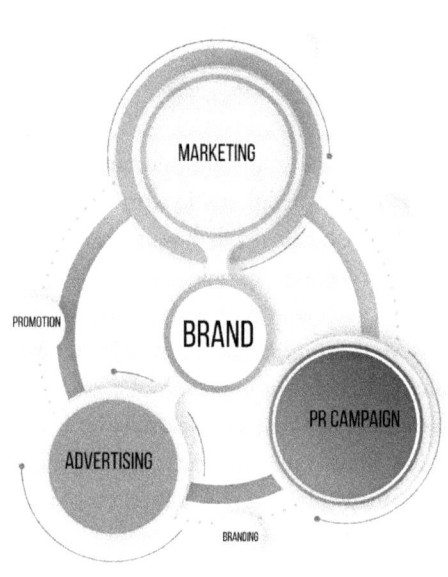

## What is Promotion?

In marketing, promotion refers to a different sort of advancement. A sales promotion entails the features of a particular product or service —via advertising or a discounted price. Product promotions can also be classified as "sales" or "specials."

## What is Advertising?

Advertising is the act of creating messages and using different psychological techniques to persuade and motivate someone to act, most likely to buy a product or service. Advertising is the act of communicating messages around these broad goals.

## What is Public Relations (PR)?

PR is short for "public relations" and refers to the strategic communication from an organization to the public to maintain or cultivate a public image and/or respond to public discourse.

Your marketing plan and strategy should include each term. Get familiar with these terms. Being fluent in the terminology will help you in becoming the best book marketer. Remember, you represent your book, not Amazon, not Barnes and Noble. Your book will not pick itself off the bookshelf and sell itself.

To succeed as an author, you need to:

1. **Know Your Reader Audience**
2. **Have A Brand Message**
3. **Have A Marketing Plan and Strategy**
4. **Be Consistent**

If your audience doesn't know your book exists. How do they know to buy what you're selling?

If you are a/an:

- **Self-Published Author**
- **Aspiring Author**
- **Emerging Established Author**
- **Author going through the publishing phase**

Do not wait until you get the physical book in your hand to market.

**Chapter Takeaway:** Marketing begins well before the publishing process.

**Chapter Affirmation: I WILL CREATE A MARKETING PLAN STRATEGY FOR MY BOOK NOW!**

# Chapter Four

# How To Set Your Book Apart

> *"I've learned that people will forget what you said, people will forget what you did, but people will never forget how you made them feel."*
> —Maya Angelou

What will set your book apart from other authors?

Publishing the book is the easy part. The actual works begin before you receive the physical copy of your book in your hand. So far, we have covered the basic foundations of establishing an author brand.

Besides Branding and Marketing, what will set your book apart from other authors?

Here are questions you will need to ask yourself and answer before you market and promote your book:

**Do you have a Brand Message?**

 

**Does your book add value to your reader audience?**

 

**Does your book solve your reader audience problem?**

## Does your brand message include the following?

- **UNDERSTANDABLE:** Make it easy to understand what you want to convey.
- **SHORT & SWEET:** Make sure readers quickly understand what you're trying to say.
- **CAPTIVATING:** Make sure your message is unique, creative, and stands out.

During this process, you want to make sure you have the following essential MARKETING tools when creating a marketing plan or strategy:

**MARKETING STRATEGY:** A marketing strategy is all of a company's marketing goals and objectives combined into a single comprehensive plan.

**READER AVATAR (READER AUDIENCE):** This is the person or group of people you intend to reach with your book, brand and business.

**30- SECOND ELEVATOR PITCH:** It's a 30-second memorable description of what you do and/or what you sell. The goal is to earn a second conversation, not to convince the person you're talking to that they should hire you or buy your product or service.

**MEDIA KIT:** A media kit is also known as a press kit. It's a set of promotional materials to inform members of the news media to help them write articles.

**SPEAKER ONE SHEET:** A Speaker One Sheet is an attractive, single-page PDF that explains your topics and expertise, with your contact details and rates.

Remember these are things you need to have in place before publishing your book. It will save you a lot of time on the back end. If the goal for your book is to speak on global platforms, you must have these simple tools in place before you ask to be on their platforms.

If you are a consultant, coach, or professional speaker, at some point on your authorpreneurship journey, you will be asked to produce one of the above items.

To succeed as an author, it's essential to set yourself up for success.

If nobody knows you exist as an author, nobody will buy your book.

**Chapter Takeaway: Create a marketing plan or strategy that gets results.**

**Chapter Affirmation: I AM THE MOST SOUGHT AFTER AUTHOR**

I've Published My Book, Now What?

## Chapter Five

# 5 Reasons Authors Give Up On Their Book

*"If nobody knows you exist as an author.
Nobody knows how to buy your book."*
—Stephanie A. Wynn

Writing a book can excite and overwhelm at the same time. Many authors market their books to friends and family without having a plan for the book. As creatives, we get so consumed with the writing, the editing, and the formatting process we lose focus on what matters most. The AUTHOR BRAND.

Publishing the book is the easy part. The actual work begins before you get the physical copy in your hands. Often, authors will promote and market their book to everyone. What happens when the buzz goes away? Some authors give up on promoting their book, and others move on to something else.

Here are five reasons authors give up on their book:

1. **Not Clear On Your Reader Audience.** Your reader audience are the people most likely to purchase your book? It would help if you clearly understood your ideal reader before publishing.

Where are the people interested in your book located?

Are they online or offline?

Can your ideal reader afford to purchase your book?

Does your ideal reader like paperback, eBook, audible book?

These are simplistic questions to ask yourself.

2. **No Marketing Plan or Strategy.** Having a marketing plan or strategy is the foundation of success as an author.

Do you have a marketing plan or strategy?

3. **No Author Brand.** If nobody knows that you are an author. Nobody will buy your book.

4. **No Support System.** You will need to surround yourself with business-minded people who support and believe in your vision. Stay away from those people constantly telling you writing a book is a bad idea. Primarily if they have never written a book. Your support team should be solid.

5. **Lack of Confidence.** You must put in time and effort to write and publish this very thing. Your Book! Stop telling yourself that you can't be a successful author. Lack of Confidence is a fixed way of thinking.

Do you know you were created to be great, and you MUST start BELIEVING IN YOURSELF! If you don't believe in yourself, how do you expect your reader audience to believe in you to purchase your book?

And there you have it — 5 Reasons Why Authors Give Up On Their Book. Now, let's tell the world about your book by building your AUTHOR BRAND!

**Chapter Takeaway:** What is the mission and purpose of your book?

**Chapter Affirmation: I AM CONFIDENT IN MY BOOK!**

I've Published My Book, Now What?

# Chapter Six

# How To Position Yourself For Publishing

*"Your brand is the single most important investment you can make in your business."*
—Steve Forbes

If you are hiring a publisher, you want to ensure that you are clear about your contract's details and the services you will receive.

Below are questions you want to ask before selecting a potential publisher.

Does the publishing process include the following?

1. **Developmental Editing**
2. **Copyediting**
3. **Proofreading**
4. **Book Formatting**
5. **Book Cover Design (front/back)**
6. **ISBN Registration with Library of Congress**

How many rounds of edits are included in the publishing process?

Do you provide book formatting? If so, how many rounds of formats are included?

What book distribution platform will you use, Kindle Direct Publishing (KDP) or Ingramspark?

Remember, no BRAND, no BOOK SALES!

**Chapter Takeaway:** Research the terms I mentioned in this chapter so you can now be in a better position when or if you hire a publisher.

**Chapter Affirmation: I AM A SUCCESSFUL BESTSELLING AUTHOR!**

# I've Published My Book, Now What?

## Chapter Seven

# Believe In Yourself

*"If You Don't Believe In Yourself… How Do You Expect Others To Believe In You"*
—*Stephanie A. Wynn*

Everyone has a story inside of their belly and now is the time to take the time and tell your story unapol-ogetically. But before you tell your story, there are things you need to put in place before you get the physical book in your hand.

Here are questions you want to ask yourself:

Are you willing to commit to building your author brand?

---

---

What's stopping you from building your author brand?

Do you have goals and dreams for your book?

## You Must Put In Effort and Time

On this authorpreneurship journey, you will encounter many distractions. Some will be big, some will be small, but whatever you do, do not give up. Believe so much in yourself that it scares you.

Are you ready to build a solid author brand?

Have you considered investing in an accountability mentor or partner?

In the next 30 Days what are you wanting to accomplish with building this author brand?

**Chapter Affirmation: I BELIEVE IN MY BOOK, MY BRAND AND MY BUSINESS!**

As an added bonus, I have provided free Author Templates and Resources that you will need to start the process. Now, it's time for you to get out of your own way and build this Six Figure Author Brand.

# Author Terms

**Business Mindset:** A way of thinking that enables you to uncover and see problems as opportunities and then turn those opportunities into a business.

**Growth Mindset:** In a growth mindset, people believe their most basic abilities can be developed through dedication and hard work—brains and talent are the starting point (Dweck, 2015).

**Fixed Mindset:** In a fixed mindset, people believe their basic qualities, like their intelligence or talent, are simply fixed traits. They document their intelligence or talent instead of developing them. They also believe that talent alone creates success—without effort (Dweck, 2015).

**Brand:** A Brand is the physical aspect of your platform. It's the website, logo, and marketing tools such as flyers, business cards, etc.

**Branding:** Branding is positioning your platform in front of your ideal customers. It's your product and or service, the method of communication you'll use to connect with your readers.

**Marketing:** Marketing is the process or technique of promoting, selling, and distributing a product or service. Marketing constitutes the big picture of how a company plans to raise awareness of its brand and convince customers to make a purchase.

**Media Kit:** A media kit is also known as a press kit. It's a set of promotional materials to inform members of the news media to help them write articles.

**Speaker One-Sheet:** A Speaker One Sheet is an attractively designed, single-page PDF that explains your topics and expertise, with your contact details and rates.

**Public Relations (PR):** Public relations is a strategic communication process that builds mutually beneficial relationships between organizations and the public.

**Literary Agent:** A professional agent who acts on behalf of an author in dealing with publishers and others promoting the author's work.

**Publicist:** A person who publicizes, especially a press agent or public-relations consultant.

**Advertising:** Advertising is a business practice where a company pays to place its messaging or branding in a particular location.

**Promotion:** In business, promotion is **any communication that attempts to influence people to buy products or services**. Remember, Advertising and Promotion are different.

**Hybrid Publishing:** Hybrid press or hybrid publisher is a publishing house that operates with a different revenue model than traditional publishing while keeping the rest of the publishing practices the same.[1] The revenue source of a traditional publisher is through the sale of books (and other related materials) that they publish. The revenue of hybrid publishers comes from both book sales and fees charged for the execution of their publishing services.

**Traditional Publishing:** Traditional book publishing is when a publisher offers the author a contract and prints, publishes, and sells your book through booksellers and other retailers. The publisher essentially buys the right to publish your book and pays you royalties from the sales.

**Self-publishing:** The author pays for the book's manufacturing, production, and marketing and keeps all income from the sales.

**Print On Demand:** Print on demand gives self-publishers the best value per book. The cost to print a book, or many, depends on the page count of your book and the print specifications you choose.

**Ingramspark:** A **self-publishing company with a global distribution network that** allows self-published authors to publish and distribute print books and eBooks. Ingramspark's global distribution network is called Ingram Book Group. For more information about Ingramspark visit https://www.ingramspark.com/.

**Kindle Direct Publishing:** KDP allows you to self-publish eBooks and paperbacks for free. KDP will give you direct access to your book on Amazon and will enable you to create a product detail page for your book. It also allows you to expand your book's availability globally, making it more accessible for readers worldwide. Publishing with KDP gives you full rights to your book, which is not something a traditional publishing house typically allows. For more information about KDP visit https://kdp.amazon.com.

**Developmental Editing:** Developmental editing is a type of book editing that focuses on ideas- the substance of your story.

**Copyediting:** A copy editor will catch any misplaced commas, errant semicolons, and that one time you forgot your main character's nickname is Margie, not Margy. Copy editing can include making corrections to spelling and punctuation. However, the editor generally focuses more on grammar, word choice, and enhancing overall writing quality.

**Proofreading:** Proofreading is a surface-level check. It is the final check performed on a document. A proofreader will look for misspellings, incorrect/missed punctuation, inconsistencies (textual and numerical), etc.

**Book Formatting:** Formatting is how your manuscript looks and reads; it's the font size, page color, word count, page number, line spacing, paragraph breaks–everything that goes into the visual appearance.

**Bio:** A sentence or brief paragraph about the writer; can include education and work experience.

**Blurb:** The short description on book covers or book dust jackets promotes the book, the author, or features testimonials from book reviewers or well-known people in the book's field. Also called flap copy or jacket copy.

**Synopsis:** A summary of a story, novel, or play. As part of a book proposal, it is a comprehensive summary condensed in a single-spaced page.

**Copyright:** A means to protect an author's work.

**Elevator pitch:** Concise pitch for a book or screenplay that can be delivered in the time it takes to travel in an elevator.

# Author Resources

# Free Resources

To obtain more information about building an author brand, visit stephanieawynn.com

**Author Brand Awareness | 30-Day Marketing Calendar:**
A Simplistic thirty day marketing calendar for authors. This 30-Day Marketing Calendar was designed to provide authors with 30-Days of Marketing Prompts. You will no longer have to worry about what to post on your social media platforms. Grab Your Copy Now!
https://bit.ly/authormarketingcalendar

**Let's Talk Business with Stephanie A. Wynn™ Podcast:**
Let's Talk Business Podcast with Stephanie A. Wynn is an online business podcast with a mixture of branding, marketing, business development tips and special guest interviews. Discover how you can establish your business the correct way. The Let's Talk Business with Stephanie Podcast is available on all major podcast streaming platforms. Check out the latest episode letstalkbusinesswithstephanie.com/

# Paid Resources

**Jumpstart Your Author Brand Strategy Session:**
This is an intensive 1-hour, one-on-one live virtual session with Stephanie to help authors jumpstart their author brand. This exclusive coaching session takes **one** issue you are struggling with within your book, your brand, or your business and help you to turn it around.

Upon completion of the coaching session, you will have access to the recording of the session and an Author Blueprint. Do you need a solution to a problem you are experiencing with your book, your brand or your business? Sign up for your Author Brand Strategy Session today https://bit.ly/authorstrategysession.

**Jumpstart Your Author Brand Bundle:**
The Author Brand Bundle is for authors who are in need of brand awareness. Do you need social media custom graphics design for your brand? This bundle includes, five custom social media graphics, two custom carousels, and two coaching sessions. Grab your Author Brand Bundle Now https://stephanieawynn.com/product/jumpstart-your-author-brand-bundle/

## In-Person Live Events

**Ultimate Author Book Tour Masterclass: A Step By Step Training On How To Conduct A Nationwide Book Tour**

This Masterclass is for aspiring, emerging authors, where we provide the essential tools and resources needed to succeed beyond publishing. During this Masterclass, you will learn *How To Plan A Nationwide Book Tour*, Learn the Step-by-Step requirements to sell your book in the major retail stores (Target, Barnes and Noble, etc.), and How To Pitch and Follow-Up with Bookstores. To sign up for this masterclass For more information about the masterclass, visit: stephanieawynn.com/shop.

# Author Brand Checklist Template

These are the items you will need to build your author brand.

- ☐ Know Your Reader Audience
- ☐ Website or Landing Page
- ☐ Brand Colors?
- ☐ Establish Social Media Platforms
- ☐ Create Social Media Graphics
- ☐ Signature Logo
- ☐ Speaker One Sheet
- ☐ Media Kit
- ☐ Create a Marketing Plan or Strategy

# Author Book Signing Pitch Template

(Greetings Insert Name),

My name is (Insert your name), author of (Insert the title and ISBN number) and (Insert the name of your business is applicable) I will conduct a nationwide book tour in (name of the city).

Insert a brief description of your book, including a pain point that your book solves and why you would like a book signing at the bookstore.

Include how your book helps the community.

I would welcome the opportunity to request an author book signing at (Name of Bookstore and Date).

I have included my media kit here for your review. Looking forward to your response.

# About the Author

Stephanie A. Wynn is recognized as a global business development strategist, author and speaker who has coached hundreds of authorpreneurs and entrepreneurs combined. Stephanie is the host of the five-star podcast Let's Talk Business with Stephanie™ and creator of the I've Published My Book, Now What?™ Workshop Series. Stephanie has a strong desire to teach business leaders how to build a six figure author brand and business so that they generate more income beyond just book sales, which inspired her to write her groundbreaking book Readi-Set Go! A Simple Guide To Establishing A Successful Small Business. She is eager to share all she has learned over the years about authorpreneurship and business ownership and hopes to inspire others to follow their dreams. For more information about Stephanie visit www.stephanieawynn.com.

# Index

Alice Sudlow https://thewritepractice.com/author/alicesudlow/. "What Is Developmental Editing? The Writer's Guide to Developmental Editing." *The Write Practice*, 12 Mar. 2021, https://thewritepractice.com/developmental-editing/.

"Branding Definition - Entrepreneur Small Business Encyclopedia." *Entrepreneur*, https://www.entrepreneur.com/encyclopedia/branding.

Forsey, Caroline. "What Is a Media Kit - and How to Make One [+ Examples]." *HubSpot Blog*, 18 Aug. 2021, https://blog.hubspot.com/marketing/media-kit-examples.

Frost, Aja. "12 Elevator Pitch Examples to Inspire Your Own [with Templates]." *HubSpot Blog*, 16 Sept. 2021, https://blog.hubspot.com/sales/elevator-pitch-examples.

"How to Create an Effective Reader Avatar." *SmartAuthorsLab*, 10 Dec. 2020, https://smartauthorslab.com/create-reader-avatar/.

*Kdp.amazon.com - Self Publishing | Amazon Kindle Direct ...* https://kdp.amazon.com/.

LLC, Lightning Source. "Self-Publishing Book Company: Print & Distribute." *IngramSpark*, https://www.ingramspark.com/.

"Marketing vs. Advertising." *American Marketing Association*, 24 Jan. 2022, https://www.ama.org/pages/marketing-vs-advertising/.

"Publicize Definition & Meaning." *Dictionary.com*, Dictionary.com, https://www.dictionary.com/browse/publicize.

"Speaker One Sheet Template." *SpeakerHub*, 20 Aug. 2020, https://speakerhub.com/blog/speaker-one-sheet-template.

Ward, Susan. "What Is Promotion?" *The Balance Small Business*, The Balance Small Business, 3 Aug. 2020, https://www.thebalancesmb.com/business-promotion-definition-2947189.

"What Are the Different Types of Editing?" *Enago*, https://www.enago.com/author-hub/what-are-the-different-types-of-editing.

"What Is a Marketing Strategy? Definition and Examples." *Market Business News*, 4 Dec. 2021, https://marketbusinessnews.com/financial-glossary/marketing-strategy/.

# Notes

# Notes

# Notes

# Notes

CPSIA information can be obtained
at www.ICGtesting.com
Printed in the USA
LVHW022112141122
732652LV00009B/623